We The Blacks

Who We Are, What We Want and
How To Deal With Our Race

Zach Tate

ISBN-13: 978-0-9984026-9-7
The Imprint Mass Media, LLC

Visit our website at: www.TheImprintMassMedia.com

TABLE OF CONTENTS

INTRODUCTION

Race is so important to only a few. Those who have been the victim of racism has accepted the culture, or simply become immune. This book is the final answer to help the masses know who they are, and the role their race plays in society. Before I go any further, I want to thank you for picking up this book, and I especially want to thank you, if you purchased it. So how do you know if you have an issue with race? How about this, if you woke up this morning and your skin was Black, your culture was Black, and you were subjected to the treatment of Blacks by another race of people forever and feel like you would...well, kill yourself, then this book is for you.

If you feel after much debate that the statement isn't true, then this book is also for you. It is amazing that in North America we still have issues with racism, but when you're done reading this book, you will completely understand why the hatred is real. You will also understand that racism is an emotional commitment to ignorance. Many Caucasians are foolishly afraid that Blacks, Asians, Indians, Latino's, Aborigines and most of the world will do to them what they did to those people, but let me quickly put those fears to rest. The issues that I address in this book will allow you to see that the White/Caucasian people who really control the wealth of the world will destroy it before they lose their supreme power. So, sit back and let me explain what this book isn't, and *is*, truly about.

In understanding Blacks and why we are feared, one has to admit the gray areas of people. Blacks have class issues, too. The same way the upper class Whites look down on what is called, "poor White trash," is the same classism that goes on in the Black community. Currently, there's a segment of Elite Blacks who look down on someone like me because I grew up in the ghetto, don't have the right degrees and don't belong to their secret organizations. In a nutshell, I am not their kind of people. On the other hand, as a Black man, at times I, too, judge and allow stereotypes of lower class Blacks to influence my thinking, but some things are common sense. When I see a certain kind of White, Black or Latino male cruising through my upward mobility neighborhood that I pay these high ass taxes to live, I cock my hammer back and wonder why the S.W.A.T team hasn't shown up. Not because I fear my own people, it's because I'm cautious around *anyone* who has a criminal demeanor, looks predatory or is perceived as a threat, especially those in uniform. The difference between me and many Caucasians is that I cannot afford to fear stereotypes because I am oppressed by them. What would also be a surprise to racist Whites is the fact that most productive Blacks don't approve of other Blacks who consider themselves Niggers, Niggas or Bitches, and this book is *really* for you, if you think we condone that or that they are one in the same.

This handbook is an eye opener, and most Caucasian's rather prosper with their myopic vision, so if you are a White man, and picked up this book, I commend you. It suggests that you either understand that there is a systemic problem with the way North American's view race, cultures and people who look differently than them. Or, you purchased this as a guide to assist you in speaking another language, which brings me to what motivated me to write this book in the first place. Secondly, I want you to repeat the following while reading this book: Zach is not complaining or looking for your help, he is simply stating facts.

At the time of this writing, racism is the elephant in the room that people just don't quite understand. It is also a tool, used to pull at the emotional heart strings of certain people in an event to create a profitable outcome. Racism is also a safety net for those who have gained tremendously from it, and Caucasians has gained privileges of elitism, simply because they now control the media. Racism is also a silent language, used in institutions and the media daily, and as long as people are going to see race before they see another human being, then we might as well teach you how to communicate with us. And guess what? If you're a

White man, I'm writing about you! But let me now issue my disclaimer.

My skin is what people call Black. I do not consider myself an African American, a Negro and most definitely not a Nigga or Nigger. I do not believe that all the ills of my life are because of the White man. I do not use my race as a crutch, a stepping stone, or an excuse to remain ignorant. I also will not, under any circumstances, believe that another flesh and blood-filled person, is superior to me based on a status he or she inherited, or simply because they are different, or because they hold a gun, even if the court system says differently. Many who look like me, do not believe that anyone owes us anything or that we need someone else's charity to get ahead. I am wise enough to know who is in charge and to stay the hell out of their way, and I possess enough wisdom to know that life is too short to spend it hung up on ideologies and political rhetoric. So, I do not blame the Caucasian for the evils I have succumbed to, but I also won't play dumb to the wicked shit they get away with. So what exactly will this book do?

This book is a helpful guide for the reader to understand race and the way White men should acknowledge their privilege and denial. It is a guide for White men to navigate through the social and political spectrums of Blacks and Latinos. This handbook is a breath of fresh air that will poison the elephant in the room, and blow the roof off the glass ceiling so that we can all cut the nonsense and make the world a greater place. This book is also a wake-up call for the ignorant Black, Latino and Whites to realize their personal powers and use them for the benefits of everyone everywhere, instead of feeling threatened for no reason at all.

CHAPTER 1

Why You Have All the Power

White man. You may be in denial about the fact that your power is not at risk. Based on propaganda, certain supremacist conversations or the extreme paranoia of poor Whites who think "The Blacks" are going to take away their grand lifestyle, the rhetoric of division abounds and is profitable for some. But, do not fear, the Caucasians before you have created institutions that will spread the methodology of how to properly oppress others so that all power can stay right where it is.

The average man isn't naturally that bright. There's a level of competent intelligence that some strive to increase, while most utilize their level of intellect, strictly for the ability to articulate what it is that they want. This want is generally communicated by way of employment, to fulfill a desire, or simply put, beg in a nice way. All others generally utilize whatever intellect they must to socialize or just get along, and within the parameters of socializing, people either filter or choose who they socialize with based on what they have in common and what their levels of intellect are. So, if it is true that some strive to increase their intellect while others just get along for the sake of socializing, then it should be very clear that the upper-class, or privileged are trained to dominate intellectually, thus showing them how to not only increase their intellect, but also how to maintain or increase their power.

Europeans who dominate the power in the world have created Ivy League learning institutions. These institutions are created to provide an *education* to those who have the privilege to afford their outrageous tuitions—which are usually the children of the wealthy or the powerful. Prime decision makers groom their predecessors. These institutions create the modern kings and queens of the land. Everyone else is groomed to receive mass *indoctrination* in an effort to rise to the status of pompous worker bees, lifelong dependents, or TV taught sheep who are needed for the slaughter that provides the casualties for the wealthy feast, or their predator's balls. The divide between race and class in America has spread throughout our learning institutions. With the invention of more technology and the spread of school policy preparing minority children for test taking over life skills, the dumbing down of America is in full effect. The chemicals used in the fast food industry, along with the chemicals found in substandard foods that minorities scrape to afford, have been proven to cause autism, learning disabilities and lack nutrients that the brain needs to develop. Under no circumstances will a class of citizens who eat organic food and have chefs at home subject their children (their greatest investment) to eat what poor inner city kids are forced to eat. One can easily deduct that the powerful are receiving everything they need to be powerful, while the underprivileged are not only being denied a level of higher learning, but their foods are preventing them from taking the steps to any form of power.

With such dynamics in place to maintain the power structure, no matter what class or race one may be, the elite will not allow the Black or Latino to have enough power to effect change for his or her own people. Just ask Obama. He was held up as a symbol of hope to the poor, underclass and the rest of the world as an example of one who came from humble beginnings, and if he can make it, then anyone can. But the truth of the matter is, he is the direct example of my point. No matter how high he ascended, even as the leader of the first world, his hands were tied, not only by congress, but also by the Caucasians who control the wealth of the planet. His power was given and restricted by the institution of politics and the ones who control politicians.

What I described above is a sad reality of minorities. Often times they are on the bottom of the totem pole, but the person with the power isn't a person at all, but an institution. Minorities are reminded that their healthcare, freedom, education, police protection, salaries and financial aid can be taken away or compromised at the whim of someone with infant power, who often believe that due to the minorities' lack of education or resources, any injustice they receive is somehow justified. But what happens when someone who has wielded a vast amount of privilege their entire life, or the people with the infant power look just like them, or are related to them, is issuing the injustice? Often times there will be no justice served because the person with the infant power can identify with the other party, or the consequences of violating someone who may know someone with greater power may be too severe. The mere fact that Whites with infancy power can appear to have greater power, contact someone with greater power, or be mistaken for someone who holds the greater power, he or she will never receive the humbling demonstrating of negating their power. The system works for them because it was designed for them, and for those who mimic or resemble the elite.

Due to the indoctrination, lack of intellect and proliferation of stereotypes, if the average Caucasian was the victim/benefactor of mistaken identity of the powerful, can you imagine how a chance encounter could result in eternal wealth for that person? The fact that one can even be mistaken for someone who makes the decisions that can change the world automatically makes that person appealing, employable and non-threating. If he or she speaks well, can represent a brand based on their level of indoctrination, then that Caucasian gains entry through any door he or she wishes, for the most part. Based on the traditional hiring policies of the Caucasian, such as nepotism (your family member hooked you up or you work for a family business), word of mouth (your social group of intellects hooked you up), executive head hunters (after your first hook up you learned how to pad your resume so that you're attractive to hiring scouts), or the good old fashion job interview (where, as we already went over, if it's you getting the job so your overall racist and paranoid soon-to-be Caucasian employer can feel at ease, or a minority getting the job, we already know who's getting the job), when White has always been right, no matter how far from the truth that may be, how dare a White person in America, or anywhere else in the world that the Caucasian has invaded, be worried about losing their power?

The elite who control the power of the world have children. Those children have family members and friends. Those friends have social, educational and business networking clubs, fraternities and social villages that always need new participants. Although this also applies in the culture of the Black elite, that Black or Brown skin is still, in 2017, a red flag that will stop them from effecting world power. But for a Caucasian, I hope I clearly explained how you are born with a foot already in the door. If you need a road map, let me explain.

True Power

The races only have issues with each other because of power. If you have the power, you control the flow of money; and, if you control the flow of money, you have more freedom in the world, and on occasion, the freedom to impose your will over the will of millions of people. The White race has demonstrated that they will maintain power at all cost and this really pisses people off, especially the people who rely on someone else to validate them. If you're a poor White man, right about now you're scratching your head because you're seeing just how poor you have it and you're wondering why the hell everyone else think you have it well based on the color of your skin. You're also a direct example of how White supremacy is a lie, but it created a perception, and that's all most of the indoctrinated world needs to know. Are you still skeptical? Well, let me tell you a story and explain to you how a few little White men feed that perception in an effort to keep what little power they have.

Let's say you live in a single house in a valley. You ventured out of your area and ran into a man and his wife who left Texas and are now hungry and homeless. Your compassion rules you and you decide to take this man and his wife home. You give them food to eat, a hot bath and the clothes in your closet that still has tags on it. After you eat, you sit around with your new house guests and sip cognac by the fire and you realize, you know what? I'm going to let them use the back room, after all, it's a big house and you and your wife will appreciate the company. The next morning you wake up early with enthusiasm. You're going to go out, go fishing and hunting because you want to have a huge feast to welcome your new guests. But when you get back to your house, your houseguest is sitting at the front door with a bloody meat cleaver in his hands. You find out that he killed your children, raped your wife who got pregnant during the assault, and he signed over all your property into his name, but offered you a small lot of it, but you must pay a mortgage and tax on what used to be your land.

The story above is pretty interesting, isn't it? Well, that's the story of what the Caucasian has done *everywhere* and to *everybody*, consistently all over the world. It wasn't too long ago that the Caucasian came down from the mountains of Europe and into what they renamed and called Africa, in an effort to survive. But while they were there, they attended all the schools of higher learning, learned how to cook with fire, speak, make medicine, bury their dead, utilize the stars and examine the planets that these darker people originally came from (yeah, I just wrote that), only to wait a few generations to come back and wage war on the same exact people who gave birth to their nation. Then a few hundred years later, another set of Europeans got lost and came here, found more Africans that they named Indians, only to kill off all of them and enslave the others in an effort to secure world domination. Then they changed the native's customs, culture, faith practices, sent them to boarding schools and gave them European names. Thereafter, they convinced the world that all slaves came from Africa, so making them indentured servants and property for the span of their lives wasn't so bad. Finally, they made it illegal for anyone other themselves to gain knowledge that would make them self-sufficient and the moment a group of people prospered in any way, White men waged war on them to keep them oppressed.

The oppression of others in an effort for the White man to get ahead is an evil tradition that has been passed down from one generation to the next. Now in the modern age, some poor, ignorant Caucasian believes that all people are poor because of choice, even though they are the descendants of those who reaped the benefits of the wars, rapes, slavery and human violations. Why? Because White people take care of their own. They have to. They truly are the minority, so if things hit the fan, they can band together and control the armed forces who will further oppress the people who helped them gain their wealth. This is what Blacks call, White Privilege. If we all agree that there are people who are under-privileged, then we must agree that some are over-privileged. White Privilege is not to suggest that Whites don't work hard for what they have. It simply means that in many ways you're beyond the cloak of suspicion, you benefit from government policies, the police and the media assume you're innocent until proven guilty. Lastly, no matter what socio-economic background you come from, you can clean up nicely, sliver your way into affluent networking clubs, villages and secret organizations, and then reach no limits. But allow me to help you understand how deep this privilege can go.

A Black man in America is born suspicious. If you're out in public, at your job or place of business, or meeting the parents of another Black person, you're suspicious. Why? Some will argue because the poor will do what the White man has done and cause harm to strangers to survive so they have to keep their guards up. Others will just admit that they fear the unknown and anything that they don't understand. Yet the truth of the matter is the media, from the beginning of broadcasting, has always made the darker man a threat, a servant, the boogie man or a beast of some sort. The handful of small White men who make big decisions for the rest of the world promote and reward separatist behavior. As a matter of fact, keeping people distracted with their social or racial differences allows them to divide and conquer and create more wealth. Is it ever going to change? Of course, we will all be speaking Latin soon, but in the meanwhile, if the Caucasian pays attention to this book, he or she will not be able to say that they no longer know why other races have a problem with them. Like I wrote in the introduction of this book, it's all about power and how you benefit from it.

The Power of the Government

So what exactly is our government and who controls it and why? Well, after a few historical massacres, the Caucasian made it very clear that they would create a government of wealthy land owners who would create customs and traditions for all the poor people who depended on them to follow. The more these plantation owners created industries and those industries spread throughout the United States, those customs and traditions became law. So who was going to sign up to enforce those laws? The poor white men. Some form of power had to be given to them because they were living in the same deplorable conditions as blacks and foreigners. So in an effort to make them feel equal and not rebel or kill the wealthy whites, a few things happened. At first they were given status and great salaries so that they could also afford to own people as property, which instantly allowed them the benefit of all oppressive governmental policies. They may not have owned plantations, but they owned slaves, and that gave them immediate identification with the wealthy plantation owners they worked for.

These same poor Whites, after acquiring land and benefits, quickly realized that, although they were given more benefits than Blacks, they were still under the control of their employer's. Suddenly they started to identify with the ills, suffering and hardships of the Blacks because, if they opposed the wealthy plantation owners, then they would be fired and lose their land, slaves and the benefits of government policies. So what did the wealthy landowners do to make them feel equal? They started using the term "Caucasian" and "White man," and writing them into governmental policies which allowed those who fit that description to be granted millions of acres of land, for free, simply because they were Caucasian. These governmental policies also gave the average White worker at the time the freedom to take the property of hard working, mis-educated Blacks. The more the term "White" was used, the more Blacks were demonized. Once Whites saw the financial benefits of demonizing Blacks, and how the act of doing so could mean the difference between being poor and wealthy, not only did the Black family become an enemy of the state, but they were valuable for labor, free property and allowed Whites to live out any form of demonic torture they could come up with because the Government promoted laws that declared Blacks to be less than human. Now that we are hundreds of years removed from such open practices, the government hasn't changed those traditions and customs.

Blacks and Latino's are undervalued in the court system and the government supports those practices. I won't take the same remixed arguments of why two million Blacks and Latinos are incarcerated, when together, both groups are not the majority of the U.S. population. What I will say and probably repeat throughout this book is, if one is not considered suspicious, then they could never be a suspect. If one is not a suspect, then he or she will not be detected for a crime, and if they are not detected, then they can't be arrested. If they're never arrested, then how could they become incarcerated? But let me give you an example:

Little Andy grows up in a rural town. He and his buddies used drugs, drag raced down the road and then snuck in a neighbor's barn. While high on heavy narcotics and dosing off with a lit cigarette in their mouths, they set the barn on fire, burning it down to the ground. When the law is called in, who is showing up? Before I go further, I want you to be honest with yourself. What was your image of Andy? Did you automatically minimize his actions because you *thought* he was White based on his name and rural upbringing? If so, you already deemed Andy exempt from being prosecuted. But let me explain how it really works. When the law shows up, chances are the officers are White like Andy. They recall when they were Andy's age and think of ways to give him a break instead of prosecuting to the full extent. Chances also are that the officer, if not one of Andy's family members, he personally interacts with, went to school with, or works with one of Andy's family members. So when the investigation is done, there's an overwhelming idea of, "Why mess up the kids future over one simple mistake," so Andy's parents are going to get called in and some form of compromise or negotiation is going to be made. But if Andy were Black, and I don't care if you're the Whitest of White men, you should know that Andy, and the agents of the government (The police), are going to put Black Andy in prison or give him a criminal record. Why? Because many Caucasians feel that there is power in numbers, and if Black Andy goes to prison, then there's one less person who's threatening their power. They are right when it comes to power in numbers, but Andy could never be a threat to the government.

To further illustrate how the White establishment will keep their power at all cost, let's recall how Congress treated the President of the United States of America, Barak Obama. Although I disagreed with much of his policy compromising, and disliked his lack of experience as a politician, I am not blind to the fact that his race and nothing but his Black skin, is the reason why officials in the government refused to aide their boss, or the commander in chief. So if the head of the free world is marginalized, insulted, ignored and disrespected, where does that leave a poor Black child who burned a building down by accident? The truth is, governmental policies were not created to benefit poor, non-White, non-land owners, so if a White man grows up in this country and makes some wealth for himself, not only will politicians, lobbyist, congressmen and presidents allow him to change the government, but they will get behind him to be the president, despite him failing at everything else in his life. Just ask Bush III and Donald Trump.

In North America, we now live in a world where non-politicians, who have no experience in politics, spend the wealth that they could use to help others to run for the highest political office. Let me let that set in for a second… and then repeat it; non-politicians are buying their way into the running and winning the highest political position in the world, and the citizens of this country vote for them because they are wealthy, handsome, appear to be successful, and you guessed it, they are beyond suspicion. In spite of all the dirt these males who hold the same status as the founding fathers held, the poor citizens of this country quickly forgive based on stereotypes and the distractions of the political parties involved. I'm certain by now that, if you're White and reading this, you have to agree that no matter how disastrous the democrat and republican parties are, they will still represent your interest and give you direct benefits no matter your lack of participation in the political process. But with Blacks, we watched for the whole world to see, that the Black man who occupied the highest political office was ignored and marginalized, so can you image what it feels like for people of color to always feel powerless to politicians, even if they're voters? And if you think I'm crying, then ask the Black citizens of Flint Michigan.

Historically, at the onset of Blacks becoming politicized, the Republican party was probably the better option for them, but after integration destroyed their collusion, and the democrats made policies to make them welfare recipients, Blacks are still dazed and confused about how the political spectrum benefits them, simply because they won't accept that an independent party is their best bet. White Republican's power structure doesn't understand Blacks and Latinos because there is a major divide since many of them want to be White, and at the very least, gain the privilege of Whites, so they turn to you for direction and problem solving skills, and you don't know how to even relate to being invisible, so you and the rest of the Caucasians say, "Do as I do." But when you witness and feel what it means to be marginalized, you either become indifferent, or you become a radical. And isn't it a damn shame that it took White radicals to form the NAACP and other pro-Black institutions just for Black issues to be acknowledged? Are you convinced yet that your power is not at risk?

Republicans have demonstrated that they don't even know how to speak to Blacks and Latinos, or how to treat them the way they treat themselves. For them, it is easier to just stay away and dismiss getting the Black and Latino vote instead of investing some wisdom to gain an understanding. The real fear of Republicans is that, if they forge a dialog or relationship with Blacks and Latino's, they then would have to follow the methods they used with every other group of humans they oppressed, and be bound to give reparations, equal education, and change their priorities from complete capitalism to equal distribution of funds. In their minds, if they return the power to the people they oppressed or killed, Blacks would force them to live the way Blacks do now, and that would simply be intolerable—even though all nations that were bombed by the U.S. gains wealth from them. I bet you can't find five things in the room you're in while reading this that wasn't made in China or Vietnam, or isn't directly related to the banks of European nations. Another fear of Blacks is that we will do to the world what we did to sports and entertainment, if given the chance.

As for the democrats, they're not even worth mentioning because it is clear that since the 1950's, they will accept whatever scraps the White elite establishments drops on the table, and then try to pass the crumbs down to the rest of us. In the modern era, a politician who is not consulted, steered through financial gain, or "funded" by big business is considered an idiot in a cheap suit. So, if what democrats claim to represent during election time, which is usually the upheaval of social, educational, police and health care policies for the poor, are not backed by big business, they will continue to hide their kleptocracy and keep the scraps for themselves. My judgement is simply from the conclusion I formed that one is a multitude of what they tolerate, and Democrats tolerate everything that will not allow them to look radical or hostile. This political stance further helps the Caucasian because, if there is indeed a fight for power, and politics is a catalyst in assisting the acquisition of said power, as long as democrats are begging other Caucasians for power, he who has it will continue to confuse the powerless. The left wing and the right wing are all attached to the same wounded bird, and that bird sits in the cage of a very wealthy White man who will never allow that bird to fly. At least poor whites can see or pet the bird, but the Black and Latino? They will end up in a similar cage if they even try.

The Power Over Money

A Caucasian in America doesn't have to be born in wealth in order to gain wealth beyond his wildest dreams. And neither does Blacks or Latino's. The difference is, a White man can gain power from the power of his money. I don't care how many Latino's who have the money and played the game for a lifetime you find, none of them can buy a Major-League Baseball team. The same applies to Blacks in basketball. Wealth is distributed differently among Whites. It is their forefathers who set the customs and traditions of capitalism into play, and those who are not descendants of the forefathers find it extremely difficult to gain true wealth or power. What I'm writing about is not a rapper who spews ignorance and promotes the death of his people, but owns 300 million because his people supported his product until it crossed over to all people. He and his whole family can pay for the greatest schools in the world, but they will never be able to pay for the privileges of the elite. Do I believe that there has been an ambassador of Caucasians who sits above the investments of Black banks and the people who run them? No. But denying non-Whites access to purchase major

TV networks, teams, and learning institutions, denies them the opportunity to influence and change their own people, which only gives more power and sustainable power to the Caucasian.

Like I expressed in my disclaimer, I am not here to complain, look to be a victim or be angered because someone appears to have it better than me, but come on White man, if you have power over the money, schools, mass distractions that we call entertainment, and have the government backing you, how dare you believe that oppressing someone else makes you more powerful, or that your power is at stake if another race achieves wealth? Exhale, you're good, you have nothing to worry about, so stop hating me because you think I'm coming for what you have. All I need you to do is leave mine alone, don't try to take it, and slowly step out of the way while I'm coming through to exercise my ability to gain wealth. And in the event that you didn't know this, the feelings I just expressed is exactly how most productive Blacks and Latino's feel. Our belief that you're always safe and will always have power is also fueled by the one thing that we could never control, and that's the power of stereotypes.

The Power of Stereotypes

My neighborhood in upstate NY is mostly populated by Whites. I drive pretty expensive cars and speak better than most people—I don't care what the race. Yet, an

Asian couple who works or owns the local stationary store must have a memo from 1965 because their behavior towards Whites who they didn't know, versus how they tried to treat my wife and I, were completely disrespectful. Instead of flying off the handle and making an assumption, or quickly labeling them racist, I did an investigation with the Whites in the store and deduced the motive of their behavior and we both concluded that these Asians (Whose clientele are mostly veterans who probably bombed their land), acted the way they were simply because they picked and chose the stereotypes that they're fed in the media and which best suits their self-esteem. Did I create the stereotype? No! And I am convinced that there is nothing I can do to change it, here's why.

Right now some White man is saying, "Well, only if you people would pick up your pants, speak better and stop shooting up the place, then maybe we would see better images of you." My response is…if you want to see people who dress and think the way that I do, how about looking on TV and acknowledging the goddamn President of the United States of America. If having the greatest job in the world and having one of the highest recognition publicly doesn't change your stereotype, then nothing but *you* will ever change you.

Stereotypes are not accidents. They are categories and ideas we use as a tool of judgement that won't change unless you change your concept of the people you judge.

The problem with this is that people's biasness and prejudice are exercised through these stereotypes, and reinforced by their self-esteem. So, if your stereotype, biases, and prejudice is rocked by facts that change your mind, the process of change is arbitrary. That's the problem. If I control the media and the media shapes and forms people's perception and judgements, and every single image I put on film is one that puts a group of people in a light that makes them look harmful to the rest of the world, I just influenced the minds of billions of people, even if the image isn't based on facts.

Now, if I compound that with institutional racism, unfair government, police officers who discriminate with who they will suspect, detect and arrest, then *nobody* would want to be associated with you, unless they already have White privilege. In many circles an Asian will be treated worse than Blacks, because any war that America waged on Asian's, there were some Blacks in that war dropping bombs on those Asians. But when it comes to catching hell based on being a non-White, all other ethnic groups will quickly opt out, sell out or remove themselves from being considered Black, even though they are non-Whites. If you ask these non-Whites are they racist, they will tell you that they don't have that luxury because people are prejudice against them, too; but if you ask them has a stereotype created a bias or controls their behavior towards other non-Whites, they will be forced to admit that it does. If they don't, they are cowards and liars. Now allow me to show you what happens when you put cowards and liars in charge and how White men get incredibly rich from it.

Imagine an Arab walking down the road with a bag. He leaves the bag near a building, becomes distracted and jumps in a cab, leaving the bag. Don't lie, you automatically thought a bomb was in the bag, didn't you? This is just a smidgen of how stereotypes marginalize people and can get them killed.

In North America, there were citizens like the Unabomber, Timothy McVeigh, The Weather Men, and a total of 129 Caucasian home grown terrorists who attacked U.S. institutions, killed American women and children in masses, and who were mostly Christian. Yet, no one is screaming to close the borders, investigate churches, demonize poor White trash, incarcerate the families of these terrorists or drop a bomb on their communities (There has only been a handful of incidents where citizens on U.S. soil have been attacked by so-called jihadist). It is clear to me that to expose the fact that all serial killers, implementers of biological warfare, home grown terrorists and gunmen involved in mass killings all happen to be Caucasian, would undermine the power of public perception that a handsome, educated or wealthy White man is automatically good. For us to admit the evil that these men do would suggest that they are just as bad as the people the media has deemed American enemies. It may even lead to the lies in the history books being uncovered and demonstrate that the founding of America was made by terrorists. Just ask the Africans who were named, Native Americans.

The power of creating and controlling the image of the stereotype through media manipulation is a tool Caucasians have always used to achieve, maintain and accumulate more power. The psychological influence of what images on screen can do is best exemplified in the 1915 movie, *The Birth of a Nation*. This film set the tone for racial terrorism in America and created fear of Blacks. In the film, one of the first of its kind back then, the Black character was played by a White man in blackface who was obsessed with White vagina, was portrayed as a beast, and clearly demonstrated to the masses how the Ku Klux Klan should burn crosses and mutilate blacks as punishment for having a different shade of skin. Before the release of the movie, the Klan had never burned crosses or wore their white hoods and disguises that we now see in every image of them. Exactly the way kids watch a movie with fighting scenes and leave the movies kicking and practicing the moves that made an impression on them, is the exact way that whites in America followed the characters in *The Birth of a Nation* to declare war on Blacks. With the lack of innovation on the part of the filmmakers thereafter, for generations, Hollywood played copycat in promoting the image of the Black man as a beast.

Movies create images and those images form perceptions and those perceptions are accepted as fact by the masses. If I have a tool like a movie, that convincingly help millions of people discriminate and Blacks seem less than human, then I automatically make the lives of Blacks less valuable. Once I deem you a beast, it's okay to watch you get shot 52 times by trained police officers because you were reaching for your wallet to produce the identification that the police just ordered you to show. Discrimination is a status, and that status is fueled by prejudices, and those who are prejudice generally feel that people get what they deserve, and deserve what they get. So, if the media has fed you that White people are better than everyone else, if the work force shows you that the White man will get hired over the more qualified Black or Latino, and you have influence over the money, government and people's perception, what the hell do you have to be upset about? The world is yours. While you're coasting on a Segway to explore and conquer homelands, the rest of us are on a treadmill trying to catch up.

If you're Caucasian and still reading this book, you deserve a prize. These words are jarring, I'm sure, to those who are in complete denial about the privilege of being White, and I will address later in the book why, if you are White and struggling financially, it's only because you're complacent and too afraid to handle the bumps and bruises of capitalism. But in the meantime, I hope you're starting to see that in having power, it is senseless to hate, impede or promote stereotypes of Blacks and Latinos; but at the end of the day, you will eat better than we do, if we are both on equal ground. You have so much power that the Caucasians in charge of greater institutions not only control the images and perceptions of other people, but they even control our Icons.

The Power Over Our Icons

What are icons and why are they important? Well, an icon usually represents a symbol of power to a group of people who receive inspiration from the person or thing that's idolized by the masses. The person who destroys, controls or removes the icons, essentially has the way to do the very same thing to the masses. Now what does this have to do with racism and power? The direct relation is historical and relevant to how a Caucasian will have a better understanding of your own power, and hopefully understand why all other people tend to have a disdain towards you.

It would be foolish for anyone to question the origin of humanity and try to dispute that the cradle of civilization started in what is now known as Africa. It would also be equally foolish for anyone to dispute that the overwhelming majority of people from that region are extra dark people, so where did a pale Jesus Christ come from? Why are all the pictures of religious icons of people who didn't even know how to draw at the time that those icons were worshipped? Fortunately, some things can't be hidden. All throughout Europe, images of the Jesus's mother, the Black Madonna, are either carved into the Christian temples, or the parishioners willfully bow to the ancient statues. Unfortunately, Blacks and Latino's forgot where they came from and were indoctrinated to believe that *they* were the uncivilized barbarians of the past. Many actually believe that they were of Viking decent and suffer from all forms of delusional buffoonery, which only minimizes their amalgamated self-esteem, which aides to the power structure of the Caucasian.

Removing the African noses off of sphinxes, destroying the ancient relics of Nubian people and rewriting history in an effort to proliferate White supremacy didn't stop in the past. In the present, most Black icons have been emasculated or destroyed physically, financially, socially or vocationally, their reputations have been ruined. Every boxing champion of the world who was idolized by people globally, and who defied or exposed the cruelty of White men was destroyed in the above manner. From Joe Lewis, to Muhammed Ali and Mike Tyson, they were either prosecuted, exploited or attacked by way of federal financial institutions. Their defiance caused them all to be financially scrutinized in a way that was far beyond the scope of their White counterparts who were just as guilty of mismanaging their funds. If you want to truly break a man, make him broke. It is not as if other athletes, like Rocky Marciano, didn't have tax and personal issues, but those men would never receive the same consequences simply because they did not instill pride in minorities.

No matter what race or ethnic background you're from, think about it. Name an icon of African descent that wasn't assassinated, given a physical disability or incarcerated. I am not suggesting that because they were rich and famous that they should be exempt from prosecution, but I am very clearly writing that it cannot be a coincidence that every single Black icon's legacy ended in ruin. So, if you control the people's icons, and tarnish the ones that currently exist, what is left to evoke racial pride? The answer is nothing. The result of the lack of leadership and racial pride has given birth to a generation of hopelessness, and a hopeless Black man might as well be a poster boy for White supremacy, because he will never be equipped to empower anyone who looks like him or her.

The exclusion of power over their icons wasn't an arbitrary move of oppressed people, but it is a clear method utilized in the marginalization of them, making the Caucasian's fear of being defeated by Blacks and Latinos ridiculous. You are not under attack. You do not have to live in fear or be super sensitive about race because you will never have to deal with racism. And most importantly, remember that it doesn't matter who doesn't like you when you have the power. Just watch Trump, he exemplifies it.

CHAPTER 2

What is Racism?

Racism to us is when we have the wherewithal to achieve whatever we want to achieve financially, or otherwise, but the opportunity is denied to us for no other reason than our culture, our appearance, or the color of our skin. A small example of racism is when Wesley Snipes, a prominent Black actor, found loopholes in the government tax laws that allowed him to not pay certain taxes. Based on the loop holes, and some negligence on the part of his attorneys and accountants, Westley Snipes was sentenced to years in prison. Then, Donald Trump gets on national television, during a presidential debate, and brags that he's smart for not having to pay taxes. With Trump's declaration, Blacks across the nation have an overwhelming sigh and say, "Now, if Trump were Black, his ass would have been thrown in jail, or the IRS would have launched an investigation into why he wasn't paying." These types of injustices are the things that highlight racism, but the list can go on.

For one to discriminate against another based on their race is racism, and most Blacks have accepted racism as a way of life in North America. What we will never accept, and what will perpetuate the tension between races in America, is the practice of discrimination. Like I mentioned earlier, with the spending power of Blacks, the proliferation of Black millionaires can explode overnight if the media promoted that Blacks support Black-owned companies the way Jews support Jewish businesses. With the increase of wealth, all we are asking the Caucasian to do is to get the hell out of the way. If Michael Jordan, Magic Johnson, and a few Black hundred millionaires decide that a professional baseball team is for sale, and they have the cash in hand, stop denying them. Money is money, but Black money is always considered funny money, if what is being purchased will represent a symbol of power. Why?

In my humble opinion, the system of discrimination is a tradition that is passed on from the creators, and at the end of the day, we are all looking at each other with a reason to hate when the elite are getting richer while poor whites are called white trash, but the subjugation of Blacks make them feel better about themselves? The masses in America have been hoodwinked into being distracted with race while the rulers of the world are concerned with class and domination. But in case you, as a Caucasian still don't understand where this came from, let me reiterate.

The fundamental values of the British was to survive in luxury at all cost. All other cultures and civilizations were considered "barbarians" that needed to be civilized, the same exact way African's taught them centuries before what civilized living meant. When the British rulers shipped their own criminals and savages over to the new land, by the time they were trading slaves, the only value Blacks had to them were to be items that were bought and sold. You do realize, Mr. or Ms. Caucasian, the psychological disorders that had to be accepted in order to see another human being—one who was physically, sexually, spiritually and mentally more developed than you, at the same level as cattle?

Propaganda suggests that an estimate of over an 11.5 million people were stolen from paradise and shipped to a new land that did not share their customs, religions, language or culture. After surviving the hell of being transported here, their very first welcoming was barbaric torture…to *millions* of people. During and after slavery was abolished, Blacks were killed for trying to socialize with Whites, and that single handedly gave birth to the White superiority complex. Then to add the Holy Book and quote Genesis 9:25 on a daily basis to justify psychopathic tendencies was proof to these poor slave overseers that their actions were sanctioned from God. Moreover, for the laws, public policies, Executive Branch of the United States of America, medical profession and farmer's unions to all declare the Black race their enemy, or property, how do you suggest these people were going to survive? No one was allowed to assist them in living, learning, feeding themselves or using the same effort they used for their slave masters on themselves, not even the President of the country. So again I ask, how were they supposed to be victorious of this genocide? The truth is, we weren't supposed to, and *that* is the core of racism. Racists stay in a perpetual state of misery because Blacks are indestructible, and the reason the race seems invincible is because all historical evidence demonstrates that this planet was given to Blacks to maintain it and to help it prosper.

Racism to us is when we found a small patch of the Earth to call our own, and despite all odds against us, we built a community, institutions and an entire thriving industry that was called *The Black Wall Street*, but Whites bombed it and burned the homes of wealthy Blacks to the ground. Racism to us is the inability for someone to look at White racists and tell them, "You have to learn how to survive on your own and not at someone else's expense, and without government aide, like everyone else had to do." Most importantly, what we need from all Caucasians is to accept that racism exists and that you are the architects and direct beneficiaries of it, NOT so we can be mad at you and return the hate that hated us. But we can begin the healing process when Caucasians come out of denial and accept why Blacks and Latino's are still suffering the societal ills that we are. The healing and ending of racism is absolutely possible, but for it to really be taken serious, the one in charge of demolishing it has to be the same people who built it.

Ending Racism

It makes absolutely no sense for one to always discuss the problems and never discuss the solutions. As a Caucasian, if you admit that racism is a problem that will always haunt this country, and you wanted to do one single thing to help, it would be difficult to do; but if I had to choose just one thing to do, it would be to end slavery. Yes, I just wrote that. Based on the 13th Amendment of the U.S. Constitution, slavery was abolished except for those who are convicted of a crime. This small line in the constitution was not an accident, so let me explain to you from personal experience how this works.

After slavery was abolished and a lifetime passed where Whites finally began to be prosecuted for executing the Blacks that were wandering around making a better life for themselves, the White establishment needed an answer to the social issues that an entire race of disenfranchised people had to endure. They would not give land, farm, financial aid and schools to Blacks the way they did Whites with the Homestead Act. So who was left to build the country? The chain gangs. Historically, if a Black was accused of a crime, he was lynched or executed without a trial. When that became illegal but not immoral, he was carted through a court system, railroaded and sent to the prison where the descendants of the plantation overseers were the police and guards. Thereafter, whenever the wealthy landowners needed something built to help increase their wealth, they paid the warden of the prison and the warden would dispatch the prison chain gang to get the job done. Slavery wasn't abolished, it only evolved. So how is this an issue in 2017? This *same exact* system still exists.

If we go back to the story of Black Andy burning down the barn, or if he lived in the inner city and was literally captured and wrongfully sentenced like the millions of others during the 30-year War on Drugs, he would have been under-represented by legal counsel, discriminated by the judge, and harshly sentenced to excessive time that was sanctioned and promoted by the Commander and Chief of the country. After he was sentenced, he would be shipped to a prison way upstate from the inner-city, because once the government started putting sanctions on trade and farming, the farmers lost their income and a prison was built to create jobs. Those jobs were needed to replace the income from losing their farms. After Andy receives prison orientation, he would have to take a prison job, and this is where it gets tricky. Too many prisons are owned by private corporations and too many private corporations own prisons for profit. The labor prisoners provide is rewarded with slave wages, and once money is involved, too many people are invested in prisoners being slaves. If no one is committing crimes, who fills the prisons? And if no one fills the prisons, who will help to make the corporations prosper? And, if the corporations don't provide jobs to poor Whites, would that cause rebellion and anarchy?

When humans face a conflict that they are clueless about, they tend to resort to what worked for them in the past. If someone knows the past, they can often tell the future. Blacks and Latino's are the majority who fill American prisons, even though they're the minorities of the American population. This fact is that Blacks and Latinos are the new slaves. If anyone is content with allowing this modern day oppression to continue, then they are supporting slavery and perpetuating racism.

The end of prisons is not needed, but the end of prisons making profits for corporations is a devastating institution of evil. If citizens start to truly accept that every time you hear the word racism and understand the direct connections to profit, then we can put the color of our skin to the side and understand that the oppression of people has been big business in this country.

Ending racism will not come from one silver bullet, and small groups of people thrive on maintaining their illusion of supremacy, but I'm all for anyone being Pro-whatever, just as long as they are not anti-productivity and mobility of another group of people. Use your race to end racism by accepting it exists and by becoming allies with those who are oppressed.

CHAPTER 3

Who Are These Blacks and Latinos Anyway?

B lacks, Latinos, and Indians are not mutually exclusive, or any different from each other. Each group is merely African/Nubian's who migrated to a different land and spoke different languages, but all DNA, architectural, metallurgical, food forensics and etymology will show *anyone* that the origin of these groups, and humanity for that sake, started in what is now called Africa.

You've been hoodwinked. If you're the average Caucasian, you believe that African's look like the images of men that you saw in a Tarzan movie, and that most Blacks in America arrived here through the slave trade. The truth of the matter is, Africa is a continent of fifty-five countries, 113 languages, originally had more than seven different body types, and 21 skin-tones—none of them White. Another truth is, the natives that occupied other continents, such as South America, Australia, and

North America who were called Indian by the Spaniards were, in fact, African's before the place was called Africa. Now, you will ask, if this is true, how did they get all around the world?

It has always baffled me that people believe that Noah created an ark the size of a modern day cruise ship, and no one questions the validity of such a claim—most Christians accept it. So, if ship building was created way before Christ was born, then isn't it obvious the African's in Noah's time knew how to travel on the sea? Is it also possible that it was African's, who taught the Spaniards and Europeans how to build ships and use the stars as their guide, since African's taught Europeans everything else anyway? Lastly, most people don't know that the currents of the sea in Africa can push items along at more than forty miles an hour in the direction of the Americas. The people who Hollywood and Christopher Columbus called Indians (because he was lost) were, in fact, Africans. If you check the artifacts of Asians, Australians, Eskimos, and all other continents, you will discover that African's were there when Europeans arrived. Europeans' didn't invent ships. They invented slave ships. If you look at photos of the people who are named Native American's, and others from different regions of Africa; they look exactly the same.

For the sake of White supremacy, everyone in North America is given an academic curriculum that demonstrates that everyone before Europeans were savages and that all Caucasians were born dignified. Of course, we know this isn't true, but if you're a dark African on an island that's conquered by Latin speaking people who killed everyone you know for disobeying them, you would probably gladly fall in line, have his children and accept the newfound privileges being lighter skinned gives your children. So now you know how Latino's became Latino's. They, too, were hoodwinked and ignore that on their islands and continents there are darker skinned people than there are lighter. But since the images on their currency and their media were presented as lighter, and thus better, they culturally accepted that they were better off abandoning their African roots. Just ask anyone from Cuba, Brazil or Haiti. Spanish is a language, not an ethnicity. Latino means you're an African who speaks the language of colonizers. The same goes for those from the Caribbean. The culture, traditions, dances, music and food are all African. So how is this relative to the modern day Black, Latino and Caucasian? Let me explain.

As a Caucasian, if you accept how the genocide of Africans across the world has given you privilege and power, then you should readily accept why all other people have social, academic, financial and cultural dependencies on your people. And, if you can accept that, then you will no longer have to question why those same people suffer from poverty, social and economic ills and medical calamities. After all, the more of us that die or self-destruct, leaves more for White supremacist to fight for amongst themselves. But in case you don't accept that Caucasians are solely responsible for the ills of other social groups and races, let me give you another way of looking at things.

In this world, resources are not limited, but they are controlled. The greed of a handful of Caucasians would rather charge a human being $600 for a pill than to distribute the medication that originated from African plants to those who need it. Once capitalism is involved in the most human transaction like medical care, then we are doomed. But for me to yell from a mountain top that this is an injustice would only fall on deaf ears because Blacks and Latino's are already *living* that reality. So, what does a Black and Latino do nowadays to make life better or gain access to a so-called better life that offers them healthcare and a smidgen of the privilege that Caucasians take for granted? They try to become you!

Since the very beginning of segregation, all the lighter slave master's kids and the descendants of those kids, quickly tried their best at "passing" for White. Being White meant, not being Black, and who would want to live a life of always being marginalized when you can live a life where the only thing holding you back from elitism is yourself? But what was one to do if their skin wasn't lighter? They had to *always* be subjected to their progress being judged, accepted or rejected by a group of people who, oftentimes, did nothing to assist in that progress. And, if an opposing White had a problem with said progress, then the darker skinned Black would be subjected to the most demented form of torture the White man could conjure. It is my belief that this practice of torture has never come to an end. It is only hidden better, and the same victims of it back then are the same ones who have to endure it socially, politically, and economically now.

In the modern age of 2017, *no one* born after 1970 is exempt from mass media directly influencing their thought pattern. Since most media companies are owned by Caucasians, one doesn't have to guess why, even in fiction, the Black or Latino will be the first to be victimized, marginalized or cast as uncivilized. America is one giant business and racism is a fuel for that business, and most Blacks and Latino's do not want to be burned by that fuel. In an attempt to escape modern calamities, many Blacks and Latino's try their best to be Caucasian. They lighten their skin color, wear weaves that resemble White Hollywood starlets, and the so-called educated ones have taken on a tone and articulation that removes any ethnic indicators. They move to rural neighborhoods in fear of their own race and won't hesitate to take the White man's side of an argument, just because. These types are suffering from a racial identity crisis and some don't even know it.

Just think of what it means to hate yourself because you were born Black and Latino. What type of social dynamics have to be in place for a person to hate themselves based off of the color of their skin? If this isn't testimony to White privilege and supremacy, then I would be hard pressed to find a better example. Now let's examine the mindset of someone who hates people who look just like them. Latino's have bought into the labels others gave them like; "Spanish, Hispanic, Afro-Latin," and anything that removes them from being what they see in the mirror—Black! Some Blacks create new racial and ethnic groups like "Blasian," to remove their heritage. Now we all know that you can't create a dominant from a recessive, thus the reason why two Whites could never produce a Black child, but a Black mixed with anyone can reproduce that same looking race, so to try and hide their blackness is impossible, but that won't stop them from trying.

The result of the African diaspora isn't more evident than in the observation and insanity of African people putting themselves in sub-groups and adopting the labels that their torturers called them. To witness the sales of hair weaves, blonde dyes, contact lenses, skin whitening creams and the plastic surgery for straighter noses climb into billions of sales in 2016, is a marvel within itself. The identity issues of Blacks and Latino stem from them not being able to accurately pin-point what part of Africa they came from, the removal of their artifacts by their colonizers, and the criminal sanctions one had to endure in history, if they practiced their customs. But for a massive amount of people in the modern age to reject their history and run away from their culture at all cost, should leave the Caucasian feeling at ease and enrage conscious Blacks, but it doesn't. Not on a massive scale. People are too busy worshipping the media images of success, creating debt over materialism, and thinking the American dream will give them escape from their roots. So to ask these groups of people to unite and equalize the socio-economic conditions by supporting each other's businesses is nearly impossible. They do not identify with anything that isn't validated by Whites. So why would a Caucasian fear a group of people who has forgotten who they are and readily accept the culture of Whites as their own even though Whites show them that they will never be accepted?

As a Caucasian, the self-identification of Blacks and Latino's is only relative to your reality if you're interested in labels, stereotypes and addressing your fears, but for the Caucasians who are still scratching your heads about these people, and want to know "what is their problem?" let me briefly give you another glimpse through the eyes of these so-called minorities.

The Ku Klux Klan. This is a White supremacist, terrorist organization and militia that falls under the banner of Christianity to promote power to Whites in America. Now think about the Ku Klux Klan. Allow all the cross-burning images, lynching, castrated bodies and political leaders of the organization that television has fed your mind. Remember that they are never prosecuted.

There has never been a war on American terrorist. The Klan is accepted and allowed to protest and have their own broadcasting and media propaganda in all forms. Now take a deep breath and clear your mind. Slowly imagine if a group of people from African descent did the same exact thing, but they yelled "Black Power," or "Kill Crackers," "Allah U Akbar" or "The Black Man is God!" If you squirmed in your seat, felt uneasy or fear invaded your entire being, it is my premise that there lies the problem with most Caucasians in the world. They have a privilege that came from the oppression of others, but the thought of others doing what they do in an effort to love themselves, it causes dis-ease. Many Caucasians feel that we do not have the right to be right, that our views are never valid and that our safety is only at the mercy of their whims.

For Caucasian's it is better for Blacks and Latino's to stay confused, hate themselves, declare urban war on each other or forget who is creating the policies that aide in their oppression. Blacks wouldn't have time to kill Blacks in Chicago if those men had the jobs that were shipped to China. The Caucasian *should not* be held accountable for the current choices of adults, but it would be beautiful if they stayed out of the affairs of those who try to help themselves. When minorities unite to declare that they want better drinking water, the end to a pipeline that destroys the earth, or protect and create an organization that brings awareness to the fact that police officers, who are paid to uphold the law and protect the citizens, and are killing unarmed Black men, we ask you to stop being so afraid that your fear creates a bigger problem. For *anyone* to be offend with an organization that yells, "Black Lives Matter," is a clear indication that they don't believe that Black lives matter. It is also a clear indicator that many do not want Blacks and Latino's to unite for anything, or to express their political views, run for office or do anything that doesn't benefit Whites or support the stereotypes that Whites have.

The modern day Black and Latino should not be the focus of the Caucasian's fear. Your fear should be in why YOU sit back and allow an environment that causes people to have to protest about their human rights.

CHAPTER 4

Rules for the Caucasian

I'm sure that many Caucasians will automatically be taken aback by the fact that they have to follow rules, or that a Black man could give them a set a rules to live by, but it is obvious to us all that there are some simple things you struggle with. After all, if Caucasians didn't have a problem with race, the whole racism issue would be moot. But since we live in a world where people can't live with our differences, allow me to shed light on some things that Blacks and Latino's want Caucasians to know.

Rule #1 - Be Opened Minded

If days go by and your mindset doesn't grow and develop you into a new being on a regular basis, you are simply…stuck. If seeing someone's skin color makes you feel you are superior to them, then you're not only stuck, you're pretty foolish. As I've explained before, it would be almost impossible to ignore the stereotypes that influenced your thinking, but being open minded removes your ignorance, opens you to new experiences in your business and personal life, and most importantly, removes the obstacles that could deter you from gaining more status, wealth and privilege in your life.

I think you're more than the color of your skin. I think deep down inside you know that we all eat, shit and breathe almost the same. We all want to build a better life, destroy the negativity in it, and protect our families from harm. And, if we're extremely honest, we will agree that no other race, ethnic group or nationality is truly a threat or enemy to our existence. There has only been one race of people who has caused difficulty on all other races, and since you're already Caucasian, you are protected, so why not open your mind to those who pose no threat you? Try it, I think that you will find that having an open mind invites more wisdom, and more wisdom gives birth to your life improving significantly.

Rule #2 - Exercise Your Empathy

Empathy is the feeling of understanding or to share another person's experiences or emotions and feelings. So imagine if all of history demonstrated that your race was captured, exploited, and continues to be oppressed by another group of people for the purpose of them gaining power and wealth—forever. Let me make it easy for you; let's say you woke up Black and didn't kill yourself because of it. To demonstrate the greatest empathy is to literally walk out of your home and pretend you're Black. Only then will you be able to see the prejudice, the cloak of suspicion that others have for you, along with the way you are denied equal access to acquire wealth, even though you can afford to buy whatever you want, but your skin creates a barrier. Yes, walk out of your house and ask yourself what millions of people do when you're being served, mistreated or handled with indifference when you want to spend your money, "Are they doing this because I'm Black? Is this a race issue, or is this person mean to everyone?" Then consider how being Black is so burdensome that your worst form of abuse may come from another Black person. If that doesn't have you empathetic, view the host of social experiments where two people are put in the same exact situation, but the Black person is always handled incorrectly based on the way society views us.

The demonstration of the empathy that I'm suggesting is also a silent one. It's not to be announced or put on show like an internet challenge. It is one where before you lash out your hate or criticism, you take a step back and automatically put yourself in the shoes of the other race that you would usually criticize. It is the act of evaluating how hatred has affected those people, and where marginalizing them gets them. Then I suggest that you create a discourse with them to see how they operate in the confines of race, not in a prideful display like they should, but see their endurance, shame and stigma they receive based on something they can't change.

Rule #3 - Don't Use the Word 'Nigger' — Ever

Not only will this rule help you to not get hurt, but it will also open your mind to being more empathetic and lead you down the path where maybe you can stop seeing race when you see others, or at the very least acknowledge that, if you're not a part of the solution, then you are the problem.

The nigger word is one of the few words that automatically brings up a tragic historical narrative once it is used. No matter how many rappers use it, no matter how many Caucasians who grew up with, live, and even married a Black person gets a pass in using this word. The damage, fueling of oppression, the genocide and foundation of the Black holocaust all shared the evil of the word Nigger. The word allowed others to declare us their enemy. It identified us as less than valuable, so killing us was okay. Nigger is so deadly that Blacks know damn well that we shouldn't use it, but we watched so many people on television be rewarded for using the word. We watched a group like Niggas With an Attitude gain wealth and be promoted in the media and systematically remove positive rap from the airwaves because it fit into the agenda of White Supremacy. We see the cultural indifference that powerful Whites who control our institutions have towards the use of the word, so the proliferation of it continues. Is it a Black issue to be dealt with? Well, just imagine if the media allowed the promotion of the words, Kike, Spic, Jew, Desert Monkey, Arab, Cracker, Devils, or Chink? If you felt uneasy about reading those words, then you just got a smidgen of the feelings we have when those of us who know better hear the word Nigger. I don't care how many rappers you love while you're up in the club, don't use the N-word, or stop using it if you do.

Rule #4 Call Out Injustice When You See It

A Caucasian, with a tattooed face, studs all over his body and dressed like a vagabond is walking down a Seattle street creating a disturbance. The police show up, exit their cars with smiles on their faces because they find him comical. They approach the man professionally, but he then starts yelling, "If you come near me, I'm going to kill you." A crowd gathers, the man becomes more erratic, but the police never ever draw their guns. They don't see a gun on the man, so their guns remain holstered. Now I ask, what would happen if the same situation would have occurred if it was a Black man? You know damn well those police officers, in most situations, would have exited the car with Tasers or guns drawn. You also know that cops desire to use the weapons they have on them, and are "just waiting for the right one," to act up. So, even though big drug dealers, gangsters, home grown terrorists, serial killers and members of the KKK have all been Caucasians and demonstrated that they are a danger to all citizens, the Black guy will get shot and killed, not because he's a greater threat than the first guy. He will lose his life because his life has been systematically been devalued. That is an injustice.

Because Blacks and Latinos have been oppressed and continue to be victimized by White Supremacy, the fight against injustice can only be seen as valid once Caucasians get involved. Your active participation doesn't require that you join the Black Lives Matter movement, but it would be nice if you call out injustice when you see it. Even if it's only once a year. Even if it's because you're a little stressed and feel like yelling out your aggression at someone who is doing an injustice to not only Blacks, but to anyone anywhere, your outcry will help the issues to be resolved or removed. Hopefully, if you have an open mind, and utilize your empathy, you will accept that calling out an injustice when you see it is not a White response, but a human one.

Rule #5 - Acknowledge Ignorance

Racism is a serious commitment to ignorance. Have you ever really listened to the rant of a racist? Have you analyzed their rhetoric? These are not smart people. The smart ones are the ones who create poor food, lack of housing and lack of jobs to oppress minorities, but for this rule, I need you to acknowledge the ignorance of racism. The invention of this social construct was a ploy on the part of rich landowners to make the poor Whites feel better than the slaves, since the poor Whites lived in similar circumstances as the slaves. Now that racism is used as an identifying marker to spew anger on others physically, socially or through institutions, people are hating people simply because the others look different than they do. Which basically means a bunch of strangers are hating a bunch of strangers that did nothing to them, pose no threat, nor have they committed an act of aggression. Do you see just how stupid this is? If anyone has the right to spew hatred and evil, it's the people who are being oppressed, yet the real oppressors are laughing at us all because they are busy building pipelines and disrupting the ecology of the planet while racists are just simply...mad.

To acknowledge the ignorance of racism allows the aggressor, or the racist, to take a look at their values and hopefully to wake up to just how stupid they are being. For one to remain ignorant because it's comfortable, socially accepted, or because they enjoy dumbing down is essentially the main issue. We as the human race are just too comfortable with racism, hatred and injustice. Case in point, Hip-hop. It's the only music and expression of art where Black males are rewarded for promoting the death and destruction of their own race. It is the epitome of ignorance, sort of like the theme music for the most ignorant invention known to man, and these are Blacks demeaning other Blacks, but the people cutting the checks of these rappers oftentimes are not Black people. That does not let Blacks off the hook for their ignorance. We all sit back on the sideline as if some ambassador of justice will come along and rectify the ills of our society without our participation. When we turn a blind eye to ignorance and injustice, we are telling each other that racism isn't our problem when ignorance can not only destroy the moral fabric of our society, but it can also get us killed. Acknowledge the ignorance and refuse to participate in it. It may be difficult at first, but practice makes perfect.

Rule #6 - Dating Our Women and Men

Due to the original film, *The Birth of a Nation*, America was indoctrinated to believe that all Black men are obsessed with the pussy of a blonde haired, blue eyed woman. Due to the media promoting stories of Black males being lynched because they said something nice to a White woman, many White women believe that all Black men want them, and many Blacks proliferate that the White woman is the "Black mans' kryptonite." These are myths. We all don't want your women or men, and no matter how much your friends discuss the sweeter the juice of the black berry, I am certain that all White men do not lust for our women; if they did, racism would be stomped out overnight. In my experience, most men want sex from anyone, anywhere and don't care about race, creed or color. When it comes to a long-term relationship, well, that's something altogether different, and I find that Caucasian's need to know some simple facts when it comes to dating Blacks.

If you're a resident of North America and date outside of your race, I commend you. The issue of your union and the judgement of who you love is a burden you bare daily. Some say you can't chose who you fall in love with (I beg to differ), but if you are adamant about dating Black, what I need you to accept is that we are not all mad at you because you do. Some of us look at interracial couples and feel betrayed. We wonder if the Black person in the relationship has forgotten the centuries of hatred and oppression Whites have issued to us. Others wonder if the gorgeous Black woman is just a pet.

A few years ago, a trend in New York started where wealthy White males were courting Black women for the sake of novelty. It was expressed to me that, "They're just as expensive as a dog, but that dog can't give you head and the best sex of your life." When we see a Black man with a White woman, we immediately check his posture and silently wonder if he's fucking his way into White privilege, her pockets, or does he love the lack of "drama" that all Black women are supposed to have? If he's an athlete or someone we see as an authority or celebrity of some sort, we silently think her White skin is a status symbol. If he has no swagger and immediately puts his head down in shame when passing us in public, we know he's the pet, or was so privileged as a child that he doesn't even relate to the Black experience. In essence, he doesn't even believe he's Black, so some of us *do not* resent you when you date certain people from our race. So much so, that when we see you in public, we silently say to ourselves, "Thank God he or she went over to the other side because we don't want him or her representing us anyway."

So what are your rules? Because you're dating a Black person, it doesn't mean you have killed the racism you have been indoctrinated with. It also doesn't mean that you get initiation into the race or can become an authority of Black issues due to the person you're dating. The person you're dating doesn't speak for all Black people because guess what? We are people, too. We come from all different backgrounds, education levels, classes and ethnicities. Just like I'm constantly reminded that the members from *Duck Dynasty* or "Honey Boo-Boo," doesn't speak for all Whites, and neither does Donald Trump for that matter, then the Black race will like you to acknowledge that Obama, Lil Wayne and Steve Harvey doesn't speak for all of us either. You will never be able to have the Black experience as a White, but you will experience being with a Black person, and those are two different things.

If your interracial union produces children, please be advised that, if anyone has a drop of Black in them, then yes, we consider them Black. And yes, we know the entire human race came from the Black man and woman because through generations and mate selection, I can create a child who looks Caucasian, but a Caucasian could mix with whomever he chooses, and you will never create a dominant from a recessive, but that's beside the point. The point is, raise your children like children. You don't have to bring them to the 'hood in an effort of injecting the Black experience—it doesn't work that way. Do not confuse class with race. They're millions of interracial communities across America catching the same hell of poverty. What separates them is skin color once they go outside of their community. The best course of action when raising a Black child is to be truthful to them about racism and how it may or may not impact their lives. Be honest about the hate in this world and then hand them this book; it will help on so many levels.

Lastly, when dating people from our race, examine their culture. Fortunately, and unfortunately, in the entire world, the majority of people are of darker skinned. So when we are all classified as Black, people from other races try to lump us all in having the same social experiences, and that's foolish. You can best understand your mate by understanding how they are wired and what their attraction is to you and your skin. Because, at the end of the day, your skin may not have a damn thing to do with why they love you; but if we don't do something about racism, it will always be an issue.

Rule 7 - I am Not Your Black Interpreter

If you're a Caucasian who has no contact with Black people, and you can't understand why they do the things you see on television, and you feel you're cool because you have one Black friend, stop coming to us to interpret the actions of others. It pisses me off when someone walks up to me and asks, "Zach, what exactly did Lil Wayne mean during his Nightline interview?" WTF am I, some kind of mind reader of ignorant, drug induced rappers? Because I can relate to gang culture, the streets and Hip Hop, makes me more experienced than the person who hasn't had the same upbringing. But what it doesn't do is make me an expert on assholes who have been rich since they were teenagers and yet wish to convince themselves that an FBI indictment for Organized Crime is a badge of honor. We don't know why people do dumb shit. Every gangsta that I know would smack the hell out of Lil Wayne for being rich and trying to go to prison. In the streets, and just like White gangsters from years ago, the goal is to legitimize yourself and allow your wealth to protect you from prison, so don't ask me questions about people who have a steady diet of cough syrup. The questions that Whites ask is the equivalent of me walking up to a random White man and asking him what causes other men to be racist, eat human flesh, or get sexual gratification from a woman defecating in their mouths. Ask me about me and stop approaching me like I'm an interpreter of all Blacks, please.

Rule #8 - Accept Criticism and Fight Your Defensiveness

White fragility is where Caucasians are super sensitive about any criticism they face, not on race alone, but on anything that points out uncomfortable truths. It is a phenomena where Whites will label a powerful group of positive activists a terrorist organization just because they cannot relate. Your fragility is directly tied into your privilege where *anything* that makes you have to hold a mirror to your ancestors is automatically dismissed or demonized. And when you're angry, the people of power who looks like you will kill an entire town just to see you smile again—this is dangerous.

The social dynamics of White fragility stems from Caucasians who do not accept the fact that, during the construction of the North American society, the foundation is filled with cracks. The racial disparities only benefit one group of people on this entire planet, so why wouldn't White supremacy continue to be promoted and upheld? It's a power move. However, within that system of power, the people who benefit from the power, become too fragile when the evils of the system is pointed out. They even become hostile when someone other than them strives for their own independence and power. White supremacy is so ingrained into the subconscious of Caucasians that their conditioning finds it surprising if a non-White, who is not an athlete or entertainer, achieves success. They also believe that pro-Black means anti-White, and the truth of the matter is that they feel anyone except themselves has the right to have an outcry against injustice.

The arrogance of White supremacy allows you to minimize, negate or be in denial about social injustices, like White policemen gunning down unarmed Black children. Your perceived and actual power in this world, simply based off the color of your skin, affords you the luxury to pick and choose what requires your activity and outrage; for instance: Blacks watched as a baby fell into the arms of a helpless gorilla in the zoo, and when that gorilla was unjustly killed, Caucasians where unanimously more outraged about that gorilla dying than unarmed Black men with their hands in the air being shot down by so-called trained police personnel. This selective outrage for injustice has historically told Blacks that Whites do not value us, and they will mind their business concerning issues that don't tear at their heart strings, and that's okay. We only ask that you equally mind your business when it comes to *us* trying to take care of *us* when we form, protest and organize. We also ask that you follow this rule and resist your defensive urges by continuing to not respond to things that don't affect you, like racism.

Rule #9 - Don't Dismiss Our Rage and Violence
Non-Whites are forced to accept that the NRA is a predominantly White organization because White fragility would create media and national outrage if dark people opened gun ranges and embraced the gun culture of America the way Whites do. Caucasians also become greatly disturbed when dark people loot, riot, and set ablaze the businesses that don't respect us or our capital whenever we set them ablaze due to an injustice that we all feel deep in our moral core. Lastly, when we handle our disputes with fist, knives or guns; Caucasians dismiss it as animalistic and want us physically dead, or socially dead, by locking us away with life sentences without ever

examining what conditions that forced us to the violence. So let me explain:

Poverty means lacking resources or having less than. Less than in education, health care, employment, nutritious food, sexual education, drug rehabilitation, academics, police protection, government grants, equal protection of the law, home and business ownership, and spirituality, to name a few. The conditions of poverty are once again dictated by the elite and the fact that one percent of our population owns most of the wealth of the entire world, combined, is a clear demonstration that poverty in the inner city is something that the rich, White elite can do something about. But instead of building community centers, or affordable housing, they support gentrification and close community institutions to build more Trump towers. Without privilege and respected representation, where are these people supposed to be able to have their grievances addressed? Not only is their food, clothing, shelter, and all hierarchy of their needs put at risk based on the conditions of their environment, but their livelihood is always under attack, whether it be legal or illegal. Such treatment and disenfranchisement creates frustration, and that frustration is exacerbated with brutality, and eventually that anger must be released.

Oftentimes, inhabitants and victims of crime are subjected to being victimized by people who look just like them. White on White crime cannot grow into a mass proportion for two reasons. If biker gangs waged war on each other, the media wouldn't frame the war as a war, but would minimize it as "disputes." It should be very clear to every American that the media and news journalist has a slant when it comes to their description of offenders who have darker skin. Just watch the evening news. A Caucasian can kill all the inhabitants of an entire Christian church and we will not hear about his criminal history, his parents won't be demonized, nor will his picture stay in the news for over a day. But in an effort to promote stereotypes and maintain White supremacy, the media will even demonize darker skin *victims* of an unjust crime. The other reasons White on White crime will not reach an alarming rate is because Caucasians are valued more by authorities and everyone from local law enforcement to the C.I.A will address a White on White massacre as a national problem and quickly wipe it out. Of course, crime is crime, but the way crime is reported has everything to do with how the public perceives the action as either violent, or tolerable. For Whites, even their horrendous crimes are not immune to their privilege.

During the 1920's when Prohibition was enforced and gangsters were running rampant throughout North America, these ruthless gangs were Europeans who became notorious from killing other Europeans. The Italian Mafia, the Irish gangs and the Jewish mobs painted the inner cities of America red with the blood of their own. Did we read about America minimizing the value of all those lives that were lost due to White on

White crime? Did America feel it was okay for all these men to kill entire families over greed and then dismiss it as only an urban problem for poor people from urban areas to fix? If you don't know the history, let me help you. Almost every single urban development program, institution for delinquency and welfare was created to address the social ills of Whites and the inner-city Irish immigrants who were blamed for almost every deplorable act in the news. The solution the White establishment created to address these social ills was jobs through labor unions, municipalities and federal aid to small business owners. Will they ever do this for dark people at the same rate they did for European immigrants?

If the injustice, poverty, and violence that dark people are forced to contend with, or be immune to, wasn't dismissed by the Caucasian bureaucracy, the answer for inner city ills wouldn't be mass incarceration, less funding to education and White criticism. Either use your privilege to call out the existence of Black genocide, or silently accept that the only people who truly have an issue with the death of dark people, are dark people, but please do not dismiss our rage, understand it.

Rule #10 - Don't Deny Your Privilege of Being White

Caucasians have colonized the entire world through genocide, waged wars for greed, and produced famine to put the exclamation point on White supremacy. The victors who benefit from the spoils of war that was waged on humanity are those who look like the masters who control the wealth of the world. From generation to generation, nepotism and favoritism has paved the way for all Whites and made them completely immune to the institution of racism. If no one blocks your progress, you will always have the red carpet rolled out to your path of pursuing all your desires. Accept it.

CHAPTER 5

Everyone is Someone Else's Nigger

As you should know by now, the use of the word Nigger was meant to devalue people's lives. If I devalue you, and see you as less than human, then I can justify enslaving you for labor, relocating your family, stopping your income, or even killing you. During industrial slavery, after intense fear was implemented into the psyche of a man, he allowed himself to be enslaved in fear of death, and held onto hope. To wealthy, White landowners, these "niggers," as they called them, were seen simply as an employee, but humanly reduced to less than a man so the slave masters' warped sense of morality could remain intact. The same goes for a modern day employee in the culture of industrial capitalism.

Let's use White Andy as an example. If Andy grew up in a rural town in the heart of America where everyone survived from farming corn, and due to America's demand for corn related products, Andy and the generations before him were able to survive and produce wealth for their family. Suddenly, the U.S Government hands down subsidies and issues mandates that regulate the production of corn due to some new foreign trade policy that his local politician helped broker to line his own pockets. Now that no one needs Andy's corn, what is Andy and his family left to do? They receive a form of welfare, or they appeal to their government to help. The government then turns to the private sector and convinces an entrepreneur to drop a factory in Andy's town to provide jobs for the labor force who used to be farmers. The pay will be lower than farming, but due to fear of starving, and the hope that something else will come along, Andy and his family goes to work at not only building the factory, but working on the assembly line as well.

Years go by and Andy and his family has made the most of the wages they make in the factory. Another politician who participates in Crony Capitalism—where the politician lines his owns pockets with government money by organizing businessmen to get government contracts—comes along and decides that there will be better relations with China if the factory was moved there. Furthermore, a decision is made that the current factory to be manned with robots and computers in order to keep up with the production of China, causing massive layoffs and poverty to wreak havoc in Andy's town. In a matter of two years, a thriving community was reduced to a crime ridden, drug infested slum where property values plummet and local government has no aide to assist the community they serve. What those politicians and businessmen did to that entire, predominantly White town, was treat them like their niggers.

Angry, poor Whites who bought into the fantasy that their skin color was supposed to give them wealth without ambition, work, or innovation on their parts, are often the archetype of hood wearing Ku Klux Klan members. What none of them realize is that their anger stems from them being treated like niggers by capitalism and their government. What the elders of these people know is that on the plantation they were treated the same way, and the master of the plantation has been replaced by big business. But what they fail to accept, no matter how much its shoved in their faces when they go to the bank, is that slavery, the use of the word nigger, and someone telling them that they were better than slaves even though they were living in similar conditions as the slaves, is that it has always been all about Big Business!

It doesn't matter how White you are or how privileged you may think you are. If a robot or a child in a foreign land can do your job better for less wages or no wages at all, your life is meaningless. The same exact way the slave master didn't care about the consequences of compromising the life, livelihood or culture of his nigger, is the same way capitalist don't care that you will no longer have health care, be able to feed your family, or maintain your culture when they close the factories, because to them you are the modern day nigger.

Chances are, Andy and everyone in his town are not greatly educated. They don't have the ambition or skill to just pick up and move, just like the slave couldn't. Andy and his family are filled with hope that something will happen for the better, just like the slave did. In desperation, Andy may even turn away from the wealthy man in town sleeping with his wife and daughter if it means food on the table, or for them to survive and stay in good graces with the wealthy man that allows them to sustain, just like the slaves had to. And lastly, if Andy's child is diagnosed with cancer, since the factory (coal mine, prison, farm, military base or any other business that feeds White American's in rural towns) is closed, they have no health care. At that point, his old boss, his KKK brothers, or his hatred of Blacks won't do a damn thing to save his child's life. If he had affordable health insurance, even that wouldn't matter, because Andy has no job and can't afford anything but food.

This story of Andy is no fictional story. Across America, capitalism, politicians and the free market has wiped out jobs and the livelihoods of hard working White men and their families. Yet poor racists really believe that they share commonalities with the elite of the world. When entire industries crumble based on government policy, and a man cannot feed his family, I ask him to eat his hate for breakfast, because racial hatred is simply a distraction that allows men to vent and keep their mind off of the real culprit that causes their misery. And the true rage of these poor men, who have been mistreated and financially devastated, is that the sad truth hits them and they don't like to admit that in capitalism, everyone is someone else's nigger.

CHAPTER 6

Your Fear is Foolish

To me, F.E.A.R is a False Evaluation and Assessment of Reality. It is something made up. A figment of people's imagination and oftentimes found to be totally unnecessary. White people's fear of dark people stems from the propaganda that created the institution of racism in the first place. To believe that darker people are your enemy, opposition or your competition, it is the equivalent of standing a toddler against an adult and putting them in an Olympic race. It is useless, especially when your people sponsor the race, will judge the race, and throw an obstacle in the road just in case the toddler is the world's fastest child. What strikes me as most interesting with people in general, that means all people, is that the media has fed us stereotypes of people who are criminals, yet it has always been a White man with blue eyes and straight hair who has done the most damage across the entire world. If anyone who steps into an elevator that should be feared, it's not the man who may snatch your pocket book, it should be the man who will kill your entire family, church, or state building. It should not be the petty robber that put your defenses up, but the broker with the smile that will destroy the life savings of your entire town. I am not your enemy.

Some Whites fear that their comfortable position on Earth will be taken away if Blacks gain power. Ignorant White Supremacists were actually spreading the word that President Obama, once elected into office, would mobilize and create concentration camps for White people. Do your history, and you will see that never in the culture of dark peoples' warfare have they marched thousands to their death, brutalized children, or killed their slaves due to an act of disobedience. Dark people have proven over and over again that they are a forgiving and peaceful people, and the only time they have practiced the contrary, it was always fueled and funded by European greed.

The other fear of Whites is that dark people will seek retribution. In my experience, I am completely convinced that the greatest fear of Whites is that they will have done to them what they have done to so many others, and again I will say that that is also a figment of their imagination and here's why:

White supremacy is systematic. It has changed and controlled world history, the education of darker people around the world, the media, the entertainment industry, and the social and political spectrum of almost everyone. With such a system in place, people have forgotten that the only race is the human race, and that in times of survival, race will go right out the nearest window in an effort for us to live. However, Caucasians have the luxury of picking up and putting down this view, if they are the ones who are gaining from White Supremacy. So, to suggest that the *billions* of people who have been brainwashed into *knowing* that being White has its privileges, and to suggest that some form of retribution can take place where those privileges will be revoked, will only end in Armageddon. Every nuclear weapon in the world will be launched simultaneously before the handful of rulers of the earth will allow their power to dwindle or disappear to anyone other than their people. So what is there to fear?

White supremacy has caused so many dark people to love the White race over their own, even when the Whites have repeatedly shown that they are there to oppress. Just ask the Latinos who try to hide the fact that they are African, and forbid their children from dating an African American. Try to convince an elderly Black woman that her child could bring home someone darker than her, and see the repercussions. Lastly, the Black bourgeois would probably create a purge or some form of ethnic cleansing of their own people before they allow their investments in White establishments to fail.

Blacks have been taught to hate their heritage, culture, skin color, and themselves. It didn't take a professor teaching a lesson in a lecture hall that holds billions for this to happen. All that was required was one slave herder with an ax, chopping off the heads of an entire family in front of others to convince them to board a ship. All it took was a pregnant slave girl being lynched, the baby cut from her womb, and the overseers stomping the head of the newborn that fell to the floor. Or maybe it was the display of the Sunday town hall meeting and tourist attraction of the celebratory "burning a nigger alive," while the Whites sang, cheered and bid money on who would be granted the fine task of cutting off the victim's genitals. Perhaps it was even the perpetual compromising of Black leaders, the death of Black radicals, and the lack of funding towards any educational system that raises Black consciousness—which is the most deadly form of warfare. For centuries, Caucasians have been at war with darker people for the sake of greed, and half of that time, darker people have been at war with themselves for some form of identity. Asking dark people to harm Whites on a massive level as an act of retribution is the equivalent of asking all Whites to accept the truths and tragedies of racism; it's something that will never happen.

This phenomena of White being right and the effects of White Supremacy isn't a national view. Internationally, the Caucasian has always been the minority. All across the world, the presence of the original people cannot be removed. Pick a continent, and you will see that the original inhabitants are dark people. Asian, Polynesian, Aborigine, African, Latin and those from the Caribbean are not Caucasian. Nevertheless, the invaders of these lands have left their presence, their ideology of chasing wealth and abandoning morals, and influence the cultures to mimic the West. You pick a place and I will show you how the wealthy people of those places are undergoing surgical procedures to look whiter, and how they are slowly being demonized if they don't adopt the lifestyle and way of life of wealthy Whites.

Your fear is foolish, most people want to be you. If you don't believe me, try one day of living life through the lens of a Black person in North America and you will quickly run back to the comfort of your privileges. Everyone has your back and no matter how much you declare yourself the enemies of dark people, many of those people will ask you for forgiveness after you harm them. Yes, you can unjustly kill their child, and they will blame the child. So kick your feet up, stretch out and enjoy the ride.

CHAPTER 7

Are You Racist?

As a Caucasian, you know very well that elite Whites rule the banks, military, and governments throughout the world. At this point it should be very clear to you who has the privilege of creating stereotypes through their media outlets, and that White supremacy works for those who have White skin. If you can fight your cognitive dissidence where Whites preach, "Freedom, justice and equality," yet benefitted in every single way from industrial slavery, which is a direct contradiction to what is preached, then you must conclude that racism benefits Caucasians. The concept of people yelling, "White Power" is a bit comical when your people already have it all. To remain indifferent on the fact that Whites generally didn't invent anything, built anything, or suffered any mass calamities from any other group besides other White supremacists, should compel any human being to accept that our North American society harvest racists. Does this mean every White person is a racist? Let's see.

Racism is associated with power at the expense of all other non-Whites. Racist views are a learned behavior that's attached to an emotional belief that Whites have to be in charge, have to come first, and that they are superior to all others. Race is the division of non-Whites based on the people's distinctive traits. Racial bias is when a person treats someone negatively or different based on their race. The use of the term, "White man," was used by rich, plantation owners who wanted to show their gravely poor and mistreated Caucasian over-seers that they had something in common because their living conditions were slightly better than the slaves. If the slave drivers woke up and realized that the plantation owner saw them as another type of nigger, then another device besides race would have been needed. But since race is here and needs to be confronted, then let's be clear about the motives behind why we still feed this institution, and why we don't hold accountable the players who devalue humanity for the sake of their own illusions of power.

The privilege of being White is directly associated with Caucasian's gaining something. The perception that their benefits are at risk of being lost if Whites embraced Blacks can only mean fear is overruling reason. The call for racial separation is a fantasy. It is an adolescent impulse where the separatist hasn't fully thought out that if they are the only ones left on the earth, then that would mean they will be completely responsible for building, working and taking care of themselves. Never in the history of the modern world does White people, as a whole, know what it means to build a nation on their own. Go ahead, imagine a world without the contribution and labor of Black and Brown people. Again, this form of thinking is not well thought out, but it is given credence do to the fact that if any White person yells loud enough, they will receive support no matter how ignorant their causes are. But let me be very clear:

Unlike most people, I do not believe that the *average* White separatist is complete a racist. Moreover, I am not threatened by White pride or those who scream, "White Power." Most of them are confused, gravely poor males stuck in adolescence and will never have any true power, so they have to scream it out to convince themselves that they matter. If I had to hate a group of people, it would be ignorant people, no matter what skin color. If I had the ability to fear another man, it wouldn't be a cross burning, poor man that one bullet could put an end to. My fear would be of the males who control entire militaries and have the power to create biological warfare, famine and genocide while smiling in the face of the presidents that *he* put into power. The thought of racism without power attached to it reduces these emotions to simple biases, and we all have them. But for a Caucasian in North America, it will be terribly difficult to put his or her biases to the side if it meant they would stop receiving preferential treatment. It would be equally difficult for a White man whose love of his life is a Black woman, to forfeit his power to her or any other Black person. Inside the essence of his being will be constant conflict because he was raised in a society where the foundations of White Supremacy tells him that he has the entitlements and privileges that she will never have.

Prejudice, Biases, and personal dislikes are something that everyone possess. Judging others based on stereotypes is an act that is fed by the media, and anyone who is born after 1965 has a central nervous system that is directly connected to the images on television. If stereotypes cause you to express your personal power to stop another person from progressing based on their race, then you, my friend, are a racist. Yes, if you denied someone a job, failed to look at the resume because their name alone conjured images of Blacks being less than, then you are a racist. Lastly, if you do anything that decreases the health, wealth, and education of another person based on the color of their skin being different than yours, then you're a racist. Racism is directly associated with POWER. Anything else is just a commitment to ignorance because, what may come to a surprise to many, is that there are people who are Latin, Polynesian, Asian, Aboriginal, Tasmanian, African and many other nationalities who suffered genocide at the hands of Europeans, yet even they have a dislike for Black Americans. Are they racist? No, they are just mad and ignorant to their media brainwashing.

As I wrote before, the power of stereotypes is controlled by those who control the media. The truths are very clear that Whites controlled the masses with media propaganda that helped them tell history, form school curriculums, and provide entertainment that tells the world that Blacks are inferior and it is best for someone to be racist. Unless you wish to remain in denial, you *must* admit that there has to be some level of entitlements to Whites if every other group of people they encountered were oppressed, murdered, suffered genocide or were colonized. If you're a Christian, your bible tells you where the Garden of Eden is, that Adam was Black, that Moses had to be Black to live with a Pharaoh, that King David is described as being Black, and based on location and linage, that Jesus could not be what Michael Angelo depicted him to be, or he and everyone else with White skin would have died from skin cancer and many other effects that the sun has on Whites. So, if one has the privilege to create and promote stereotypes and rewrite everyone else's history, why wouldn't racism be fueled by those who need to feel superior? The question is, do you, the reader, support these stereotypes and the institution of racism?

Ending Racism

For the most part, racism is the act of taking your biases a step further and supporting a social system that allows injustices and oppression on a group of people whose skin color is different than yours. Skin color isn't race. The only race in this world is the human race, and some of the humans have a learned behavior that's fueled by a commitment to fear and ignorance. Like any other habit that becomes a part of someone's character, the same way one learns to be committed to a thing, is the same way one can make a commitment to remove themselves from people, places and things that support racism. I am not suggesting that extreme measures be taken like every Caucasian running out and hooking up with a Black person to rid themselves of the fear. What I am suggesting is that one rewires their psyche to stop seeing race, stop identifying others by their race, and remind themselves that their fears are foolish. But what happens to the benefits that White supremacy gives to Caucasians? Aw shucks, those benefits will roll on forever, so much so that you don't even have to put any effort into receiving them if your skin is White, so use them to end racism. Or at the very least, instead of remaining silent when you see and injustice against Blacks, speak out because your skin color makes your voice louder.

Now after all this writing, and all the reading you've done, some people are still in denial about their biases and racist tendencies. A simple test to determine if your psychological wiring isn't racist, just imagine waking up and finding out that you were a Black woman. I'm going to let that sink in. Now, the mere mention of, "Black woman," should have conjured thoughts of those you know and possibly hang out with, and if you're the type that often says, "I have a Black girlfriend," chances are you're a prime candidate who needs rewiring. But if you live in a White world, and don't interact with Blacks often, I'm willing to bet an image from a media outlet is your reference point. And that image of a Black Woman scares you, or makes you feel inferior, oppressed, marginalized or makes you squirm in your seat, then White Supremacy has done its job on you to feel better than another group of people simply because your skin doesn't look like theirs. If your skin is a few shades lighter than Black, and you weren't born a Caucasian or with White skin (for your technical types who read Caucasian and thought of geography) and you deceived yourself to believe that you're better off than Blacks, then you, too, have been doubly hoodwinked and feed White supremacy in the worst way. So what do we do to fix your programming?

The first step is to admit the evils of White supremacy and accept the historical narrative because it cannot be removed. Accept or do your research that the cradle of civilization is Africa (Whites named it that), and that the majority of people who are from there have skin as black as ink because they were the chosen people who were given the earth to have as their own. Even to this day, they are a peaceful, giving and forgiving people who allowed the doors of oppression to open simply because the group of people who came from the Caucus Mountains begging for food were people that came from their loins. God, the universe, or even science, if that's your belief, gave us an Earth with food on the ground, in the trees, running across the land and swimming in the waters. The *only* group of people in the history of this planet who had a problem with killing, destroying and altering the people, climate, culture, food and worshiping of God, were Caucasians. The obsession with greed and power led them to wage war against humanity all throughout the world. Whether it was creating war in Africa, killing Jesus, the Brits massacring Tasmanians centuries later, trying to rid the world of the Moors, the genocide and reconstruction of the so-called Native Americans as the warm up to do the same to African's in America, or the modern day destruction of the planet, extremely wealthy Caucasians have made it very clear that they don't like it here on earth. So once people accept what happened in the past, and admit who gave birth to the term race in an effort to oppress others for wealth, then and only then will they be able to see how racism in the future is an evil that will only lead to the destruction of all.

America was founded on the genocide of the African's who were named Indians or Native American by their oppressors. The profit driven culture created a division that caused Caucasian's to foolishly live in fear that, what they have done to all others across the world, will someday be done to them. If we are to end racism and make America great again, the injustices in education, medical care, food supply, policing and job opportunity to *poor* people has to stop. Because the day poor Whites wake up and finally see that they have always been someone else's nigger, is the day humans can start focusing on doing things for the sake of humanity. And once Caucasians practice taking care of humanity, all humans will benefit.

Blacks have proven that we as a people are indestructible. We do not need a hand out to fix our issues. We don't need Caucasians creating a New Deal for African Americans. Reparations would be nice, but for wealthy Whites to empower the same people whose poverty keeps them wealthy is a unicorn we gave up on riding. What Blacks need from those who want to make America great again is for others to move out of our way. Not because of your fear or greed, but because "truth, justice and equality," should not be monopolized by one race. If we have the freedom to demonstrate the greatness we have in athleticism, in all areas of humanity, race wouldn't matter anymore, because when you see us, you will see yourselves.

Zach Tate—America's Most Dangerous Author is a national best-selling prolific storyteller of true-to-life fiction who has now thrown his cap into the arena of educating the masses with his no-nonsense approach with non-fiction. He's the host and executive producer of the podcast, "The Great Zach Tate Show," screenwriter, advocate and Creator of God's Army, an organization to affect change by saving our youth, and a fitness guru with his brand Justalilmore Fitness. This profound speaker, entrepreneur and writer is a man of many experiences whose wish is to use his voice to change the world.

Order Form

Yes, please send me ___ copies of
We The Blacks by Zach Tate.
$9.99 per book, plus $5.00 shipping & handling.
For bulk orders, contact The Imprint at (929) 244-9460.
Mail completed order form to, and
make checks payable to:

The Imprint Mass Media, LLC
PO Box 1152, Pocono Summit, PA 18346
www.TheImprintMassMedia.com

Shipping Information:
Name: _____
Address: _____
City, State, Zip: _____
Phone: _____
eMail Address: _____

Special Circumstances:
_____
_____
_____
_____
_____

www.ingramcontent.com/pod-product-compliance
Lightning Source LLC
Chambersburg PA
CBHW022124280326
41933CB00007B/535